The Art of Saying Fuck No
Swear Coloring Book

Hello Awesome!

Are you ready to master the art of saying "Fuck No!"? It's easy! Just use bold, colorful language, like "Hell No," "Are you fucking kidding me?," and "Fuck off." And voila! You've got a masterpiece.

These 30 funny swear word designs are perfect for unleashing your creativity and laughing away stress. Each design is printed on a single-sided page, so you can use your favorite colored pencils, pens or markers to create fun, unique artwork.

Pro tip: If you're using pens and markers, put another sheet of paper or card stock behind the page that you're coloring to make sure no ink bleeds through. You'll find a test page in the back of the book so you can try out your pencils and pens.

Swearing is colorful language and you are a fucking artist!

Happy fucking coloring!

Jen@SassyQuotesPress.com

Do you have questions or comments? I would love to hear from you! Please email me at jen@sassyquotespress.com.

Sign up for freebies and updates at SASSYQUOTESPRESS.COM

The Art of Saying Fuck No: Swear Coloring Book

Sassy Quotes Press

ISBN: 978-1-957633-58-9

Questions? Comments?

I would love to hear from you! Please email Jen@SassyQuotesPress.com

Ready for your fabulous Bonus Gift?

Go to the **Bonus Gift** page at the back of this book for instant access download info.

Bonus Coloring Pages (printable PDF)

30 Printable coloring pages from some of my most popular swear word coloring books: *Cuss & Color, Fuck This Shit,* and *You Are Fucking Beautiful*

 Sign up for more freebies and updates at SASSYQUOTESPRESS.COM

COLOR TEST PAGE

 Bonus Gift

Hello Awesome! I hope these bonus coloring pages help you laugh and relax. This is a high-quality PDF file that you can print as many times as you like to create a variety of designs. And feel free to share with friends!

What's Included

30 Sweary quote designs
8.5 x 11 in. Printable PDF

How to Access

Option 1
Scan this QR code with your device

You will see a "Download" button for instant access

—OR—

Option 2
Type this URL into your web browser:

sassyquotespress.com/asfn30

You will see a "Download" button for instant access

—OR—

Option 3

Email me at
jen@sassyquotespress.com

I would love to hear from you! I can't promise "instant access," but I will respond ASAP!

More from Sassy Quotes Press

Check out more of our hilarious swear word planners, coloring books and gratitude journals. Available on your local Amazon marketplace.

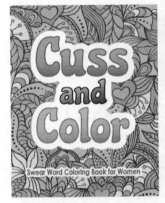

Want freebies and updates?

Sign up for free coloring pages and more at
SASSYQUOTESPRESS.COM

Questions? Comments? I would love to hear from you! Please email me at Jen@SassyQuotesPress.com

☆☆☆☆☆
A Favor Please!

Whether you purchased this book or received it as a gift...

Your star rating or review on Amazon makes a **HUGE** fucking difference to me as an independent publisher.

Seriously. I know your time is *valuable AF*. So, if you could take a quick minute to rate or review my book, I would be *very* grateful!

Two Quick Ways to Rate or Review on Amazon

 **ENTER IN YOUR WEB BROWSER**

https://bit.ly/ASFN

—OR—

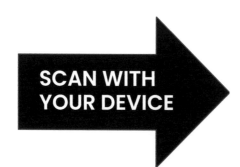 **SCAN WITH YOUR DEVICE**

Thank you! You are a fucking gem!

Made in the USA
Middletown, DE
15 September 2024

61000378R00038